# THE SILENCE

### By Evelyn Whitell

Author of

The Woman Healer; Extraordinary Mary;
The Arms of Love and Wings of Faith;
The Christmas Guest;
A California Poppy;
Shekinah

DeVorss & Co.
PUBLISHERS AND BOOK DISTRIBUTORS
843 SOUTH GRAND AVE.
LOS ANGELES

*Printed in the United States of America by*
*DeVorss & Co., Los Angeles, California*

# THE SILENCE

**W**HAT IS THE MEANING of the Silence? What is the best method of going into the "Silence"? How can I relax and get the rest I need?

These questions have been asked again and again. My reply is, that to me there is no set rule for entering the Silence, no set place and no appointed time. We can be in the Silence whenever we wish, and are in it hundreds of times without consciously realizing.

In years past, we used to think that heaven was a place to which we had to go. Every picture painted, every idea given of this home of bliss, pointed from the earth plane to the skies. Now we realize heaven is within us. Whether we are in Africa or Egypt, whether in the States or the South Sea Islands, we live and move and have our being in heaven.

Just in the same way, the Silence is not a thing into which we have to force ourselves, nor a thing for which we have to seek retirement, we can be in it at any time.

Our souls go out to our Creator on the breath of desire. Surroundings make no difference. Unity with Divinity is sought and found the moment a call is uttered. To draw down a blind, shuts out the flaring light, but it does not take us from our room. The drawing of a mental blind on scenes we do not want, brings peace and silence to the mental world whatever our surroundings.

To enter the Silence is not a strain. If we employ will power and the mind becomes active in the endeavor to get the body still, then we have no conception of the true Silence.

"Let me think" is an expression which should be changed into "Let me stop thinking," so that the Great Mind, which knows all, may bring all things to my remembrance.

If all the healings done by Jesus were recorded, probably none would be more marvelous than those at the sunset hour, when in answer to the call "Come unto Me," the sick, the weary and the heavy laden met in the golden light.

Have you ever visualized that scene? It will bring you into a better understanding of the Silence. Have you ever watched the face of anyone looking at the sunset? I recall doing this, when crossing the Pacific Ocean. The water was as smooth as glass, the white line of foam followed the ship like the swiftly moving wings of angels; the air was full of laughter and merry voices, when somebody suddenly said, "Look at the sunset!" In a moment, stillness reigned. Everyone stopped talking. Silence deep and intense fell over all, as if some radiant being, whose glory blazed from sky to sea, had suddenly bent from the golden heights, with finger laid upon his lips.

Lifted above the things of earth, faces became transformed. There was an expectancy on them too. The beauty of the scene had made all souls receptive to the power which lay beyond the golden light.

It was in such a receptive silence, two thousand years ago, that all became conscious of the never failing love which healed them every one.

## ENTERING THE SILENCE

For you who find it difficult to enter the Silence,—a good way is to call to mind the most peaceful hour of your life—the happiest moment you ever touched, the time you came nearest to heaven, when you felt God everywhere.

Close your eyes and concentrate on this, if only for a moment, or if not on this, think of the most beautiful scene you ever gazed upon. Visualize the break of dawn, when the heavens are aflame with the glory of God, and nature, beautified and refreshed by the soft dews of night, is smiling through the colors of trees and flowers.

Or, think of some wonderful painting which impressed you. The peace of the silent night, when the glittering stars smiled down on you, like the lamps of guardian angels, and the moon had made the sky a shining silver sea.

These things gave rest and joy to your soul, many a time. They calmed you when you were weary. They soothed you when you were depressed. They brought you to the hem of the garment. They wiped out by their beauty, all things which you had thought coarse and ugly.

This little story is an illustration of my point:

"A man was wishful to become a priest and teacher. He cut himself off from his friends and relatives, and went into the silence to commune alone with God. The noise of the city bothered him, so he chose the quiet of the woods. But even there he was not left alone. For, while at evening prayer, he was disturbed by a tinkling sound which passed his hut. Annoyed beyond measure at this breaking in on his sanctuary, he went to find the cause of this noise. He discovered that it came from the bracelets of a woman, who went each sunset to meet her lover down by the stream flowing through the woods. He immediately had her arrested on the plea that she went to meet her lover when she was already mar-

ried to another man. When the woman
appeared in Court, she turned to the would-
be priest, and said, "Sir, had you been as
much in love with your God as I was in
love with my lover, you couldn't have been
disturbed by the tinkling of my bracelets."

It is not difficult to concentrate on anything that we love, or on anything that has
made us happy. So as you relax, turn your
mind to scenes of joy, turn it to thanks and
gratitude, so shall you draw nearer to the
great Giver of all. So shall your soul be
filled with the peace that passes understanding. So shall you know the silence
Jesus knew. The tempest may beat and
billows roar, but their violence shall not
come nigh thee.

## AFFIRMATIONS

*I am a smiling child of love. I am wrapped in the garment of sunrise.*

*The shimmering golden rays fill me with healing power. The gold changes into deepest pink.*

*God's love is expressed through me in color.*

*Now the blue of a smiling sky shines round about me.*

*My aspiration is set in the Heavens.*

*The blue deepens into purple.*

*I am rich with the wealth of kings.*

*I turn my face to the East in adoration.*

*I believe in God the Father Almighty, Maker of Heaven and earth.*

*I see my whole body flame with His glory.*

*I relax in the white light, and on the shining rays, send out my blessing.*

*Peace to the North—Peace to the South —Peace to the East and Peace to the West.*

*Peace—Peace—Peace to the world.*

THOUGHT FOR THE MONTH OF

## *JANUARY*

*"Every day is a fresh beginning."*

I REPEAT these words and let them sink deep into my subconscious, as I close my eyes in the Silence. They fill and thrill me with new life and inspiration. I shut the door on the *past*, and, opening a new and beautiful door, I look on a fresh, clean road unmarked, untouched, a road white and stainless as fields of untrodden snow.

This road I have yet to travel, and in the joy of its possibilities I forget the things I longed and sighed for. I realize those things are not *behind* me—and I press on, knowing that they are before.

"Every day is a fresh beginning." I know I am the maker of my future. That the things I have created will meet me every hour. As God gave man dominion over all things, so that dominion lives in me. I go forth conquering and to conquer, armed with strength and unafraid.

As I still look along my future road, I get the vision clearer. I remember how the One who sat upon the throne said— "I make all things new!" I know my life is being transformed before my eyes. I don't command my stones to be made bread. I know man does not live by bread alone. I know God works His miracles in His own way. I know that as I walk with Him I shall prosper if I live His law.

The fogs may sometimes drift before my eyes, but the light that leads me is within. With a song of rejoicing in my heart I say— "The winter of my life has passed. The time for the singing of birds has come!" I pause a moment and the glory sinks into my soul.

I see the old conditions all wiped out, and from the trees which looked so bleak and bare, I see the blossoms break forth with new life. All nature is alive with joy.

I stretch my arms out, till my body seems to rise from the earth on wings. I get the vision of the conquerors, who came through tribulations great, and washed their robes so white that neither spot nor stain could blemish.

I know that in this consciousness there can be no more pain. I know God's love has wiped away all tears. I know the former things have passed away, and as I listen inwardly, the voice of ages speaks to me,—

"He that overcometh shall inherit all things." Again and yet again I say those words. I know that I shall overcome.

I open my eyes with a song on my lips. I have dropped the spirit of heaviness for the shining garment of praise. I realize how great God's love—how perfect His plan for me. I know in His Silence He has shown me that the future is in my own hands. My road is clear. It is untrodden.

"Every day is a fresh beginning." I look to this day only, to make it beautiful. Tomorrow I wil begin again, but will not ask to see "the distant scene."

Lovingly, selflessly giving of my best, I will travel onward, step by step, into the greater glory, yet to be revealed.

THOUGHT FOR THE MONTH OF

## *FEBRUARY*

*I place myself and all my affairs lovingly in the hands of the Father. That which is for my highest good shall come to me.*

My MIND is at rest as I enter the Silence. Peace, calm as a summer morning, is in my soul.

The great strong arms of the Universal Father are round about me. I relax in their strength, as one who has toiled up a hill in the heat of the day will relax under the shade of loving trees and rest from his burden.

I have lost all sense of worry for the future. I have placed myself and all my affairs lovingly in the hands of the Father.

I dwell on the word lovingly because love, being the greatest thing in the world, can, by its radiance, change all darkness into light, all sickness into health, all poverty to abundance, can lift me on its shining wings, can help me to forget and to forgive all things which in the human eyes seemed wrong.

Love cannot desire anything but what is good for its loved ones. It cannot err against its children. It wouldn't wish to see its loved ones suffer. There is no imperfection in its glorious plan for the universe. So, if I have placed myself with all my seeming difficulties in love's dear hands —whatever love shall give me in return must be for my greater gain. With love directing my affairs—I have no fear. Out of my failures God can bring success. The closing of one door will mean the opening of another.

If I cannot see the things I crave for, if the way out of my difficulties is a blank, I repeat more strongly to myself and many times aloud, "Lovingly, in the hands of the Father." I go about my work, claiming the promise for the highest good. The con-

sciousness of the love of the Father grows
more strongly on me while I wait. Into my
soul there comes the understanding of the
unity with Divinity; the connection Jesus
made for us in the blessed words "Our
Father." I no longer look for God in a far-
off Heaven. I feel Him round about me
everywhere. As a child looks to its earthly
father for its daily needs, so I—trustful as
a little child—depend on His great love,
and opening my soul to it, I feel it flowing
through me with life-giving power.

Resting in this belief I leave all my
affairs in His safekeeping and take them
not out again.

Close to my Father's love, I have the
confidence that all my future is being taken
care of—that every step is directed by Him
—that I cannot make a change without His
word—that He has promised me the Kingdom as a gift. I starve no more in a foreign
land, but I claim the bounties that it is His
good pleasure to give. When I lie down to
rest at night, I have no worry for tomorrow.

I close my eyes repeating softly, "Lovingly, in the hands of the Father." The last word on my lips before I sleep is "lovingly."

If I awake before the dawn, there is no darkness for me. Into my soul the words are whispered: "Lovingly, in the hands of the Father." I hold the statement to my heart and sleep once more—content that He is taking care of me. I open my eyes to the beautiful morning. The last thought that I took to rest comes forth to greet me with a sunny smile.

Almost unconsciously I find myself repeating, "Lovingly, in the hands of the Father" and again, "That which is for my highest good shall come to me."

THOUGHT FOR THE MONTH OF

## *MARCH*

*"God will supply my every need."*

As I RELAX and close my eyes in the SILENCE the joy of this promise enters my soul.

I feel the warming, healing love of God wrapping me 'round with an invisible mantle.

Happiness steals into my heart, and without a fear, a question or a doubt, I let go of everything, knowing that such a love as this can only *will* the very best for me, and that all my needs shall be supplied abundantly.

I have followed the statement of the Psalmist, that it is better to put trust in God than confidence in man, for although human love may fail, the God love, like the Rock of Ages, stands forever.

I know there is no lack in Heaven. I know that Heaven is round about us here. As God is my supply I cannot have an empty purse. As Christ made His demonstration from the beginning, as He claimed His at-one-ment with His father's wealth, so I being a child of a king, hold out my hands for the riches of the universe.

Like the "Silent Seventy," who trusted for their daily supply, I know that as I give I shall receive. I know the law of compensation never fails, I know that as I cast my bread upon the waters, sometime, somewhere it will come back to me.

I claim God for my banker and I will not push His hand away. He may use many instruments through which to give His scrip to me. It matters not if it should come from North or South, from East or West, it is His means of supplying my wants; it is from the universal hand.

I know that poverty in any form is not of God. The God who filled the world with His abundance, did not make suffering nor lack. I know that money is the root of good, the tree of life, the leaves of which are for the helping of the nations.

I need not worry for tomorrow. The answer to my call will come before I give it utterance.

No thought of fear can enter my subconscious mind. "Prove Me," the Lord has said, "and see if I will not open the windows of Heaven and send you down showers of blessings."

I carry this thought of wealth with me into the silence.

"In my Father's house there's bread in store." Love's hands filled with abundance are stretched toward me.

I need not stand like a prodigal outside the closed gates, when I have only to ask and they will swing back to let me in.

I visualize my Father's house, the house of plenty.

Drawn into the golden circle of the ring of love I wear the robes of prosperity. The shoes of attainment are on my feet.

I open my eyes with the sweet consciousness that my wireless has been received.
The answer is here, and that for which I
asked, I now have.

THOUGHT FOR THE MONTH OF

## *APRIL*

*"Behold all things are become new."*
—2 Cor. 5:17.

THESE WORDS sing in my heart as I enter the SILENCE.

The old condition is crossed out. Again and again I repeat, "It is finished," and I turn my face toward the sunlight of the resurrection.

Like the women who stood by the cross, I am strong in the consciousness of victory.

I await the arising of my cherished hopes. The seals of the tomb are breaking. The arms of the cross are melting into wings of light. The gift of eternal life is mine. I know that my Redeemer liveth.

I go into the deeper silence.

The stillness of the Easter morn is in my soul. I rest in the calmness of certainty.

Surely the angels of the resurrection are with me now, bringing life, health, joy and healing on their wings.

I reach out my hands so that I may feel the touch of love, so great and so divine.

I get the vision of the glory dawning over a sleeping world on the grand resurrection morning. I get the wonderful response of earth and air, when those great beings from highest worlds came down to roll away the stone and greet their Lord.

I remember how He said to doubting, fearing souls, "I shall rise again."

In this silence I plant that message in the hearts of all who see only their Calvary before them. Those who are hidden in the tomb, or those who blindly grope to find the light, I send to them the thought of resurrections. That the darkness of the night precedes the sunrise. That the tide which went back and left only barren sands shall come in bearing treasures hitherto unknown.

I feel their sensitive response to the treatment. I see the darkness melting round them. Almost unconsciously I hear them say with inspiration born anew, "I shall rise again."

Out of the silence of ages past, the voice that called to Lazarus, positive and strong, comes again with cheering conviction, "I am the resurrection and the life: he that believeth in me, though he were dead, yet shall he live." I feel *that* life eternal surging through me. The life that always lived, but which He came to give with more abundance.

I visualize all things responding to that life. The miracle of the flowers springing up out of the hard ground, in answer to the great king of light, the sun; the new sap rushing through the trees, and nature writing poems everywhere in blossom and in bud.

My soul is opening with those flowers, to let His love descend on me, like drops of dew in holy sacrament.

Just like the flowers I will trust to Him for care; content to live and serve where He has placed me; to express my life as sweetly as the meadow-daisy, asking for nothing, giving all.

*I know that my Redeemer liveth.* I know that His life redeems me from all sickness. I know that if I keep His sayings I shall not see death. My life is hid with Christ in God, and I cannot lose it. The Christ in me has risen and is alive forevermore.

The sun is shining on my world made new. It brings to light the beauties which my eyes have failed to see. I have turned my back on the tomb of the past forever. I have risen with Him, and because He lives, I shall live also.

Thanks be unto God which giveth us the victory to triumph over all things.

I go out to face the beautiful present, knowing that the future will grow in beauty just as the Summer follows the Spring.

THOUGHT FOR THE MONTH OF

## *MAY*

SILENCE FOR MOTHERS' DAY

*"As one whom his mother comforteth so will I comfort you."*

ON THIS MOTHERS' DAY I enter the SILENCE. I let the promise of the past and present sink into my soul, "As one whom his mother comforteth so will I comfort you."

As these words came to give the people a new understanding of a God they had placed in a far-off Heaven, so they give to me a fuller understanding of the vast eternal love of that great "Father-Mother God," whose eternal presence cannot leave me.

I recall how when a little child in infant sorrow I rushed for consolation to my mother's arms. I feel again the touch of lips that kissed the childish hurt away.

As the darkness of the night was turned to daylight when I heard my mother's voice, so the darkness of life's path becomes illuminated when I shut out all other sounds and listen in the Silence for the voice within— "Lo, I am with you always —So will I comfort you."

Resting in this Silence I send out my blessing, first to the women who have been given the divine responsibility of mother-hood—women who have called souls in the unseen into material expression. I give them thoughts for strength, for patience, for divine understanding, for the inner sight which enables them to tolerate and help all seeming failures in their children. For the vision which makes them see virtues rather than faults—give praise rather than blame, and to behold the beautiful angel in the soul that is struggling through the clouds of matter to attain the highest goal.

I send my thought, not only to the women who have brought children to this plane, but to the great cosmic mothers who with the vision of a new dawn can smile on the birth of any woman's child.

I visualize the future that their thought is building. I see these women the saviors of all races, drawing by their universal love all nations into one.

I send my thought to the "expectant mothers," building in the silence the holy temple for the waiting soul. I strive to lay a stone in that building when I send to her the thoughts of all things great and grand. I treat her lovingly so that she will think and talk only of constructive things. So that she will want and welcome her coming motherhood—so that peace and calm will so strongly enter her subconscious mind, that fear can find no place therein.

The knowledge comes to me in the Silence that I am a divine creator, helping by thoughts of purity and love to make a perfect child. I realize that it matters not where I am nor what I am doing I can always send out my beautiful thoughts on beautiful wings, through space. I can make the flowers bloom in the garden of some-one's life.

With the consciousness of the "Father-Mother God," my universal love shall reach the universe in blessing.

I send the thought to mothers whose children are grown and scattered far and wide. I tell them not to worry. Each child is in the hands of eternal love. Even the mother's love, great, grand, protective, is not stronger than God's. Therefore in God's love, in God's care, in God's divine keeping all are safe. .

To the mothers discouraged by seeming failure I say, "Be not weary in well doing." Be not discouraged — sometime, some-where, the results will manifest. "In due season you shall reap if you faint not."

To my own mother, on whatever plane, I send my wireless of love. I know life is eternal. I know there is no distance. I know that God makes no mistakes in His great plan. I know eternal love is endless, and wherever those we love may be, our wireless can always reach them.

I visualize the red and white carnations, symbol of this great day.

I let the purity of the white sink into my subconscious mind.

Around me shines the great white light of universal love.

I breathe in the vital energy expressed in the red.

I relax and inhale the sweet perfume of the flowers—Love, Life, Energy—I send out to the world on the sweetness of this perfume, and trustful as a little child relying on love's promises I rest content.

THOUGHT FOR THE MONTH OF

## *JUNE*

*"The sun is in my soul this perfect day."*

I ENTER THE SILENCE holding this thought. I do not ask if the weather is wet or fine. I close my consciousness to outside conditions. I see only the sun within.

I visualize that shining light in my soul. I feel the warmth creep over me in gentle waves, stealing through my limbs, and just as an awakening bird spreads out its wings to greet the dawn, so I stretch forth my arms in relaxation contented as one who rests on sunny grass and basks in the warmth of Heaven.

The sun is in my soul.

At first it seems I can only see a spark of light, small as the far away flicker of a star. Then I remember that even though my light appears so small, I am part of

that great sun, eternal in the Heavens.
One of the bright living rays shot down-
ward to the earth. I am full of life giving
force and with that spark shining within
me, my soul cannot know darkness.

Softly and joyously I begin to sing the
well-known hymn,

"Sun of my soul, Thou Saviour dear,
  It is not night if Thou be near.
  Oh may no earth-born cloud arise,
  To hide Thee from Thy servant's eyes."

As I sing I feel the light grow brighter.
I realize that if I have the sun in my soul,
my face shall shine as Moses' shone, when
he came down from the mountain. I shall
be transfigured with the glory which transfigured Jesus.

The words of Solomon come to me, "The
way of the *just* is as a shining light which
groweth more and more unto the perfect
day." If I have light in me, then I must
shine. That spark within, must rise just
like the sun until it reaches pure perfection.

I will walk only as a child of day. I will keep my mind so free from thoughts of sadness, that no spot nor blemish may dim my shining light.

Wherever light is, it always shines. I know that when the Master said, "Ye are the light of the world," He did not speak to those who sat in the highest places. He spoke to all who carry the light within their souls and let it shine wherever they may be.

Walking in the light I know no fear. The darkness and the day are both alike to me. The pure white light reveals to me the Christ in every man. With the aura of protection built around me I am safe wherever I may go. No harm can touch me when I walk in God's white light.

I realize that the stars in my crown are shining here and now. That each kind thought and loving act is adding to their blaze of glory. That I can build my

Heaven all about me, and can fill it with the light of God, and the flowers of unfading love.

I know that I am sent to take the light into the dark places. I know that my mission on earth is to help those in captivity and bondage. Therefore I must never allow myself to become depressed by the sorrows of others, but must bring my light into their darkness, and change their sorrow into song.

"The sun is in my soul this perfect day."

Each morning I repeat these words. Though the clouds may hang low over the earth, though the rain may fall heavily, the light within my soul makes all things glorious.

"Out of my aura pours the love,
  That angels breathe from heights
    above."

I pause to get the consciousness of such a love. The love which made those shining beings carry their light from worlds afar, and bring its radiance down to earth.

"Out of my aura pours the power,
    To strengthen me each day and hour."
Again I pause. My aura seems to change
to wings of light which lift me above all
sense of weariness.

"Touching my aura hearts do sing,
    And Winter's frosts melt into Spring."

I see the brightness of the light I carry,
like warming sunlight melting hearts that
were hard and bitter. Like the promise of
new birth I visualize the flowers of Spring,
smiling toward the light after being so long
hidden by the winter's cold.

"Like the white hyacinth's perfume,
    My scented aura fills each room."

I inhale the scent of the white hyacinth,
and know that I carry its fragrance and its
shining spotless purity in my soul.

"Like moonlight on a restful sea,
    My aura does encompass me."

I visualize the calmness of the waters, I
relax on the golden sand. I listen to the
gentle inwash of the waves. I know how

the beauty of the softened light can shape
divinity out of things that might seem
coarse and ugly, and I realize that if I
carry that light around me, I shall beautify
all things in the eyes of the world.

"Breathed forth by God on angel's
    breath,

My aura knows not fear nor death."

The words come to me, "I will fear no
evil." I know that evil can not touch me.
When I lie down to sleep at night I see the
light around my bed. When I awake I see
the light. I know God maketh me to dwell
in safety, and resting within this light so
clear, I draw around me Heaven here.

I visualize the great Elder Brother who
walked in the white light all the time; who
was protected by the light; and I go forth
into the world knowing that as I love the
light, and walk in the light, I shall walk in
His presence all the time, and like Him I
shall become all light and all illumination.

The sun is in my soul this perfect day.

THOUGHT FOR THE MONTH OF

## *JULY*

*"I, if I be lifted up, will draw all unto me."*

As I ENTER THE SILENCE I feel myself lifted on the wings of the spirit. The joy of the spirit is that it knows no bondage. It cannot be chained. No prison can hold it— no walls can encompass it. In spirit, I am free to go where I will, and no hand can detain me.

Just as a bird soaring into limitless space, rises above the smoke and noise of the city, so I, lifted above the noise of earth, rest on the heights that Jesus knew.

I remember it was on the heights that He made His great at-one-ment; that after He had spent the night in prayer upon the heights, He was able next day to walk upon the water; that when lifted up to that high spiritual plane, He lifted the five thousand with Him, feeding them with the bread that satisfied all hunger.

It was on the heights He delivered His most heart-searching and soul-inspiring sermon, and it was when His disciples were lifted to the heights with Him that their spiritual eyes were opened to His glory.

If I then, be lifted to those heights, nothing will be impossible for me.

On the heights I breathe the clear air of the morning. I look on the colors of the sunrise, and healing warmth steals into my heart and soul.

I feel I am myself a radiant sun, and just as the sunlight draws the flowers from the earth, the blossoms from the trees, the fruit from the ground, so if I let my light shine, I can send healing rays into every home, into every lonely heart, into every prison, into every hospital. Like the glorious orb of day, I can shine over the whole world. As I relax in this consciousness, I see the sunbeams breaking the clouds of life

on every side.  God's love is smiling
through.  It is expressed in the shining
colors of the sky.  It smiles out of my eyes
and through my lips and in return I feel
all people smiling with me.

A city that is set on a hill cannot be hid.
It attracts those who live in the darkness
of the valley.  They lift up their eyes to its
beauty, and their steps turn from the
gutters to the stars.

In the sublimity of these heights I can
walk amidst all seeming imperfection.  The
prince of this world can come but find
nothing in me.  No outward conditions can
worry or disturb me.  I take no thought
for tomorrow.  The promise was "It is your
Father's good pleasure to give you the kingdom."  I know all things are in that kingdom, and being lifted up I draw all unto
me.

Divinely poised in God, the silence of the
heights is in my soul.  I bring sweet peace
in the brightness of my aura.  The sick feel

it and are made well. The distressed feel
it, and lift up their heads.

I worry no more over the lives of others.
I remember the promise, "As the mountains are round about Jerusalem, so is my
love round about my people."

I see the One who stood upon those
heights, stretching out arms of love. I
hear the voice through countless ages say-
ing, "Arise—Thy light has come."

I realize the kingdom is here and now. I
let my light shine like the star in the East
which drew the wise men to the king.

I send out the power and the glory.

I open my eyes to the consciousness of a
world which my thoughts have helped and
blessed.

"I, if I be lifted up, will draw all unto
me."

THOUGHT FOR THE MONTH OF

## *AUGUST*

*"He that dwelleth in love, dwelleth in God, and God in him."*

THIS IS MY thought for the SILENCE. I close my eyes and meditate on what it would mean constantly to dwell in God, and God in me. There have been times when, touching the great power, I have for the moment realized that all things were possible—that all obstacles were dissolved, and I saw God face to face. But I try to realize what it would mean if I always dwelt in that power and I ask how in this world of doubt and error, and strain, and materialism can I dwell always in thoughts of God? The answer comes, "By learning to love all things, all conditions, all people; for God is love."

Emerson had the right conception of this love, when he said, "When a man walks with God, his voice shall be sweet as the murmur of the brook or the rustle of the corn." In imagination I am carried into the country and I walk through meadows of buttercups, down to where the little silvery brook is rushing over the brown stones. I listen to its soothing story, the story of everlasting life— "For men may come and men may go but I go on forever."

In my heart is the consciousness that just as the brook is the mirror for the smiling blue of the sky, so I can let my soul be the mirror for God's great love. I can by my restful presence give the balm of healing to all who come near me. As the waters of the brook are caught up by the river and carried into the sea to help bear the big ships homeward, so all my thoughts are being carried into the universe to lift on waves of light, the souls of those distressed, and bear them onward to the shore they wish to reach.

I picture the fields of corn. I see the long shining leaves and the pink tassels glittering in the sunshine. A soft wind comes blowing from the South, and the gentle rustle that responds to the greeting is soft and restful as the humming of a hymn at eventide.

Or again I picture the fields through which the Master walked—the fields that were ripe with the harvest. I see the golden wheat, the scarlet poppies and the deep blue corn flower swaying in the breeze. I realize that if I have the love His life expressed for all humanity, the sweetness of that love must steal into my voice, making it sympathetic, kind and soothing as the murmur of the brook.

Now I leave these scenes where it is easy to feel God's presence and I go into the heart of the city. All that I have in my soul I must take with me.

As I close the door of my home I send this thought ahead: "Love goes before me, making beautiful my way." As love is leading me I need not take unnecessary steps.

Love's hand will lead me only where I need to go. If my work is the work of love I shall not walk with weary feet.

In love's sweet consciousness all those I meet respond to me. I go into the stores. I do not feel impatient if I have to wait for service. I send love to the one I might have blamed. Her task becomes much easier. She feels a pleasant atmosphere amid the flurry of her work. She comes to meet me with a smile. The love sent out has crept into her heart and made her service a delight.

I step on the crowded cars. I do not frown because no seat is left for me and I have to hang on to a wobbly strap, and drop my parcels while I try to find my fare. I whisper to myself, "Love suffers and is kind." I thank God there is a car to ride on, and then I look around and see the tired faces—many full of doubt, and anxious for the future. I send this thought to each and all, "Love goes before you, making beautiful your way."

I resolve to speak the good word for my neighbor now. To give the flowers of love to her while she most needs them. If her actions to me have not always been kind, she needs my love the more. As I pass her door I bless her home. I see the power of the all good within her. I know that if we would bring peace to earth we must love every individual as ourselves, for love alone will win the world.

I concentrate upon this for a while. I realize that I am just a golden link in the chain encircling the globe. I see my link made powerful and strong. I see love written over it in golden letters. I see the other links grow brighter and reflect its light. I know my work must be just to let that link shine. Whether I mix with the great crowd or keep the Silence in my room it matters not. If my link keeps its place like a bright shining sun, it will give light and strength to all.

I visualize the new built from the old. I
see swords beaten into ploughshares, and
spears into pruning hooks.

I arise. I open my doors. I walk through
my rooms repeating, "He that dwelleth
in love dwelleth in God."

I realize my house is God's house, and a
welcome awaits all that He sends to me.

I open my window, and send out to the
universe my beautiful thoughts of love,
and I know those ready to receive them
will be blessed, and brought into a fuller
consciousness of God.

THOUGHT FOR THE MONTH OF

*SEPTEMBER*

*"Rest in the Lord and wait patiently for Him, and He shall give thee thy heart's desires."*

I REPEAT these words to my soul as I enter the SILENCE. I realize that God has done me a great honor to ask me to wait until that beautiful time has come when He shall give me my heart's desire. I have held this desire so long and have wondered why His mills should grind so slowly. Longing for action I have called, "Here am I, send me." But now I know God cannot change His law because my soul is restless. I know that when I am prepared for what I want He is there to give it to me.

I realize I shall gain strength by waiting, that I shall be better able to enjoy that which I long for, when the time for it has come. Like one refreshed by a night of sleep, I shall arise with strength renewed, and shall find added power because of the long night which kept me from the sunrise.

I remember how the poet Milton said, "They also serve who only stand and wait." It was his lot to serve unseeing within an unseen world, yet, in that inner world he found the knowledge which made it easy to wait patiently *and serve*.

I think of the parable of the laborers standing in the market place. At the third hour the good man of the house came out and said, "Go work in my vineyard." I visualize how eagerly they would respond to the call. I feel I am one with them and I cannot get quickly enough through that open door.

Again at the sixth hour the call is repeated, and again I visualize the ready response.

The ninth hour comes, and the laborers still waiting, enter to the work they craved.

And then the eleventh hour, when those

fearing that all chance was over, see opportunity stretching forth her hands.

Only one hour, and then the reward is given. The man who had come at the third hour got the same as the one who had come at the sixth. And the one who had come at the sixth the same as the one who had come at the ninth, and the one at the ninth the same as the one at the eleventh.

In the Master's eyes all had done equal service. Those who had toiled through the heat of the day were equal with those who had stood in the market place ready to respond to the call.

"They also serve who only stand and wait."

So, though I am still outside the doors of the vineyard, if I wait and wait patiently, my work shall be called *great,* because I was satisfied to serve where God had placed me, till the time for the realization of my heart's desire had come.

I pause and send this thought into the restless universe, "Be still. Don't fight

God's law. Rest in eternal love, and wait, wait patiently for Him."

If it be only service I desire, if it be just to use my gift, God given, then I can use it where I am. The desolation of the wilderness responded to the voice of John the Baptist. He preached into the empty air, knowing that not one spoken word was lost.

For thirty years the world's great teacher waited, serving His time in selfless love until His recognition came.

I remember how it was after the disciples had toiled all night and taken nothing— how when weary and discouraged, with cold and aching hands they were drawing in their empty nets, the darkness broke around them, and Jesus Himself stood on the shore.

*Pause*

I believe if I serve and wait with loving patience I shall hear the voice that the disciples heard, commanding me to throw my net in on the other side.

I believe that I shall draw to me my heart's desire. The mists of doubt shall break around me and no more upon the ocean of unrest, I shall pull my boat of plenty to the shining shore.

With this vision in front of me I arise full of energy. I take up the work I disliked, the work which I thought was not mine, but I keep my eyes on the ideal, as the laborers kept their eyes on the door through which they desired to enter.

Every hour of selfless service is drawing me nearer the beautiful goal which love's hands have prepared.

I resolve to fret no more for what is not here. I will employ each golden moment with beautiful thoughts which will build themselves into my mind, and make me strong to endure until the door of my heart's desire swings open and the call of love bids me enter.

THOUGHT FOR THE MONTH OF

## *OCTOBER*

*"I will do my best and leave the rest to Providence."*

I REPEAT this statement again and again with closed eyes, and while I do so, the mountain of difficulties, which looked insurmountable, begins to grow less.

All in a moment I see that I had taken all the burden on my own shoulders, forgetting the blessed words "Casting all your care upon Him, for He careth for you."

"He careth for you."

I dwell on these words. I repeat and repeat them till I know by the calmness within, that their power has reached me. More than ever before, I realize the love of the One who has offered to lift my burden.

I think what it would mean in the material world, if when toiling up the hillside in the heat of the day, weak and weary beneath the blinding sun, some strong traveler on the path would say, "Give me your burden. Let me make it easier for you."

Out of this material picture, there arises the spiritual vision of the One who said those very words, and in a moment, my burden is lessened, knowing that another helps me in its weight.

No more will the mountain that I have to ascend, seem impossible. I will go one step at a time, repeating—

"Jesus, do this with me."

I shall feel the loving presence of the One who trod the winepress alone.

The consolation will come that I am walking with that Elder Brother, the great white Comrade, whose aura shines like the sun about me, making the darkness light.

He will understand, should my steps falter, or the stones be rough for my feet.

On this blessed guide I can ever rely, even though the path outside the light which shines around Him is vague and uncertain; even though I feel the hands of friends relax, and grope in vain for fingers that once entwined in mine; even though the voices of loved ones answer me no more.

Stronger and stronger I grow in my beautiful ascent with Him. So sure am I that I shall see the promised land. *My* promised land. The land that He will give to those who did not falter nor turn back. Who did not waver, but who kept to the path.

Each day brings me nearer the consciousness of the Golden City. Not a Heaven far away, but a Heaven all around me here, where the power of God is so great that all who come into its rays are permanently and everlastingly healed.

Oh sorrow, that seemed so hard to bear; Oh heavy affliction, I bless you. How little I realized that beneath your robes of black, you hid the glittering garments. How little I knew it was through you I should gain my wings.

I open my eyes. I am invigorated and strong. I will not fear difficulty.

I will look at each problem as it rises before me, then lovingly turning to the One who walks beside me, I will whisper,

"Jesus do this with me."

I will do my best, and leave the rest to Him.

THOUGHT FOR THE MONTH OF

## *NOVEMBER*

*"My Joy shall remain in you and your Joy shall be full."*

I HAVE CLOSED the outer door of the world, and entering into the SILENCE, I grow into the realization of the glory that *IS*.

One moment's contemplation on the joy of the Lord, and my heart is bounding with thankful praise, my soul is singing with delight.

Slowly I keep repeating to my subconscious mind, "Full of joy, full of joy, full of joy."

This joy is not a joy to come and go, it is a joy which fadeth not away, it is the joy which Jesus came to bring, the joy He carried into every home, the joy with which He filled the soul of the woman seeking to draw water from an overdrawn well. The joy which made the lame man leap, which gave new energy to those with palsied limbs, which brought life out of death, and turned the water into wine.

If then this joy remains in me, I shall carry its illumination everywhere. I shall cause suns to shine in every home. Although I see them not, wherever my feet tread, the flowers will grow. Others will follow in my path and gather to their saddened souls the joy my influence has left.

Each day is a thanksgiving day to me. In giving thanks for what I have, I forget the smallness of the things I sighed for. I begin to count my blessings, writing them mentally in my book of joy. I lay my gift of a grateful heart upon the altar, and send aloft my grateful praise.

I pause to feel the showers of blessings, coming down in God's response. I give the thanks that Jesus gave when He claimed the answer to His prayer before the thing for which He asked had manifested to Him.

If at my daily task I should grow weary, I pause and inwardly repeat, "The joy of the Lord is my strength." The power immediately rushes through me like a well of water springing up into everlasting life.

Over the road which might seem long, I walk with ease. My feet are shod with shoes of joy. I walk the way God has directed—the mountains and the hills break forth before me into singing, the trees of the fields all clap their hands.

I no longer wish the days were over. I no longer wish the hours would fly. Into each golden second, I build happiness, and as the bee draws honey from the flowers, so I draw joy from every situation in which I may be placed.

I feel rich in this consciousness. I breathe in life and love, and once more I give thanks.

I rejoice because I am alive. Because life is eternal. Because I do not know all the great things the good God has piled up for us in the millions of worlds He has created.

I give thanks for my present experiences, knowing that if I meet them all with joy, they will bring me gladness in return.

I visualize my cup of blessings full and running over. I see myself walking in green pastures and beside still waters.

I stretch out my hands with the palms upward. I am ready and waiting to receive.

I open my eyes and see my face alight with joy. I am so full of the radiant vibration that everyone receives the power. It is carried like the perfume of flowers on the breeze.

I begin this day to write my joy book. On the first page I place my beautiful experience in the morning silence.

Tomorrow I shall have something still more beautiful to write, and again the day after—until my book, like my cup of blessings, will be too full to hold my grateful praise.

THOUGHT FOR THE MONTH OF

## DECEMBER

*"I have the Courage that defies failure."*

I AM FILLED and thrilled with power, as I keep repeating these words in the SILENCE.

Armies invisible are gathered around me, and I feel I can go forth with strength undreamed of, so strong has grown my consciousness of God.

I know this power is not my own. It is the power that always lived. The power that holds the world. The power which, when once permeated, makes the frailest vessels strong.

Of myself I can do nothing, but I remember what Moses said when the voice of God called him through the purifying fires. "Who am I that I should do this deed?"

I feel the voice has called me, yet like Moses of old, I have made the same reply.

But now I remember that Moses, timid, weak and leaning, went forth linked with the great "I AM," and was able to defy failure. Even when pursued by an army, he was able to pass through the waters untouched; able to lead the children of Israel, and make the terrible wilderness endurable, because the Lord of hosts was with him.

Like Moses, I have ever before me the vision of the promised land.

I know I have been placed on this plane with a mission and I shall continue to have faith in my God-given ability, which will lead me through all obstacles to obtain my goal.

I think of the courage of Daniel, when he dared to strike a blow in the face of temporal power, and say, "I will not eat of the meat of the king's table. I will serve my God, and not worship the image," and when he dared to pray aloud by the open window.

I know that I must live what I believe. That my life must be an open book, even though it give opportunity to those who read it, to pick flaws, to find fault and to criticize adversely.

They come against me with a sword and spear. I face them in the name of the Lord of Hosts, and because the Lord of Hosts is love, my weapons therefore are stronger than theirs, and will enable me to pass them by, and go my way.

I know that every human being who ever accomplishes anything, refuses to see the Alps ahead. He prepares for victory, and goes after it.

I picture what I want to accomplish, and I say, "With God all things are possible." I dwell on the ALL because it cuts out limitation, and brings me into a stronger consciousness of the promise, "Whatsoever ye shall ask the Father in my name, He will give it you." I realize that there is not a barrier but what God's power expressed through me can break it.

I give my hand into His, and look with fearless eyes toward the future. My faith and my belief grow stronger, as I keep repeating, "I have the courage that defies failure."

Laughing at what the world calls impossibilities, I go right in to win. Though the castles I have built may, in the eyes of others, seem to fall, I know it is only because I shall build bigger and grander by and by.

I dwell in my Ark of safety, not looking at the floods, but keeping my eyes steadfastly on the rainbow in the sky, the promise of God's help written in the colors.

I know that when I am best prepared, the door of my heart's desire shall swing open, and victory greater than my highest ambitions shall be mine.

Inspired by my SILENCE and radiant with belief, I arise to inspire others with the certainty of this victory. "According to your faith be it unto you." I have the courage that defies failure!

## SILENCE FOR CHRISTMAS

*"Fear not, for I bring you glad tidings of great joy."*

I ENTER THE SILENCE this morning with the music of CHRISTMAS in my soul. I close my eyes and see again the happy pictures of the past.

Sweet memories of childhood rise before me. A little tree adorned with gifts of love. Memories golden with happiness, ringing through bells of joy and shining snowflakes. I draw this little world of the past around me, and begin to build it into the present. Once more I have my tree of love for all whom I hold dear. I light the colored candles on the different rays, send out my thoughts of healing. I know the Christ is knocking at my door. I ask Him to come in and bless my home.

My tree becomes a blaze of light—star crowned and radiant with His glory. I touch the aura of His mighty love. My heart goes out to all the world. I want to call in all He bade us call, that they may touch this love and be made whole.

My thought has travelled on the light, and drawn by it, the weary and the heavy laden come.

My room is big enough. I hold them all.

I see the little suffering children rush into His arms, and by His strength they are made strong.

He draws close to the lonely woman, and she feels her loneliness no more, for she realizes He is with her.

He comes still nearer to my tree, and as His radiance shines upon it, my eyes are further opened, and I see that all gifts crowding the boughs are answers to the prayers which He will give to all who ask Him.

With the faith of a little child, I reach forth my hands, gladly accepting what I longed for, as the gift of His dear love.

I pause to get a fuller consciousness of such a love. A love which brought the first Christmas to this earth. The vision of it rises before me. I am one with the silent night. I am awaiting a beautiful something, which I know shall manifest through the darkness.

I pray that I may see the glory that the shepherds saw. I again pause. I wait as they did, till the mighty messenger of God speaks through the silence to me, "Fear not, for behold I bring glad tidings."

Immediately I am at rest. I have watched for the star to arise in the darkness. Watched through the blackness of the night. But in the "Fear not," the light breaks in upon my soul.

I shall follow the leading of the gleam.

I shall follow the star through the desert. I shall follow it, even if its light at times is so faint, so hidden behind the clouds that I seem to miss my way, and am always detained by the roadside.

I remember there was a fourth wise man, who was not able to lay his jewels at the feet of the king. And if, like that fourth wise man, I am detained by continual service—I will do it lovingly and without complaint—giving the cup of cold water, speaking the word of cheer, remembering how He said "Inasmuch as ye have done it unto one of the least of these, my brethren, ye have done it unto me."

Every day shall be a Christmas. The Christ born anew in my heart, makes life a thing of joy and beauty.

My soul is filled with rapture. I join in the song of the angels, "Glory to God in the highest, and on earth, peace, good will toward men."

Peace to the North
Peace to the South
Peace to the East
Peace to the West

Peace to the World
Peace!

CPSIA information can be obtained
at www.ICGtesting.com
Printed in the USA
BVOW06s1416200317

478963BV00011B/48/P